THE NINE WORDS

A Story of Faith, Love & Perseverance

STEVE DUGAN

WESTBOW
PRESS®
A DIVISION OF THOMAS NELSON
& ZONDERVAN

This book is a work of non-fiction. Unless otherwise noted, the author and the publisher
make no explicit guarantees as to the accuracy of the information contained in this book and
in some cases, names of people and places have been altered to protect their privacy.

WestBow Press books may be ordered through booksellers or by contacting:

WestBow Press
A Division of Thomas Nelson & Zondervan
1663 Liberty Drive
Bloomington, IN 47403
www.westbowpress.com
844-714-3454

Scripture quotations marked NIRV are taken from the Holy Bible, NEW
INTERNATIONAL READER'S VERSION®.Copyright © 1996, 1998 Biblica.
All rights reserved throughout the world. Used by permission of Biblica.

Scripture quotations marked KJV are taken from the King James Version.

Scripture quotations marked NLT are taken from the Holy Bible, New Living Translation,
Copyright © 1996, 2004, 2015 by Tyndale House Foundation. Used by permission of
Tyndale House Publishers, Inc., Carol Stream, Illinois 60188. All rights reserved.

Scripture quotations marked NIV are taken from The Holy Bible, New International Version®, NIV®
Copyright © 1973, 1978, 1984, 2011 by Biblica, Inc.® Used by permission. All rights reserved worldwide.

Scripture quotations marked ESV taken from The Holy Bible, English Standard Version® (ESV®),
Copyright © 2001 by Crossway, a publishing ministry of Good News Publishers. All rights reserved.

ISBN: 978-1-6642-8503-3 (sc)
ISBN: 978-1-6642-8504-0 (hc)
ISBN: 978-1-6642-8505-7 (e)

Library of Congress Control Number: 2022921837

Print information available on the last page.

WestBow Press rev. date: 12/08/2022

DEDICATION

To Momma and Daddy, who taught me to love God.

CONTENTS

FOREWORD

God spoke nine words to me in the fall of 1962, when I was twelve years old. During the years since then, I have told a few people about those words and some of the miracles God did to make them come to pass.

The people with whom I shared this story told me that I should write it down. However, I never did. This past Christmas, I sensed that I would not be able to continue my work as a lawyer because of the symptoms of Parkinson's.

I prayed and asked God what I should do. The answer I got was to write the story of the nine words that God had spoken to me all those years ago. I had been hoping for something more practical.

One night, after Julie had gone to bed, I sat down at the computer. I didn't have to spend one second trying to think of what to write. The words just came out of my shaking fingers onto the computer screen. I did the same thing every night for a few weeks. The result is what you now hold in your hands. I don't think I wrote it; I just think I wrote it down.

If you read this true book and discover that God had a plan for my life, you must know that He has a plan for your life, too. If you come to the conclusion that God loves me, there is no reason for you to doubt that He loves you just as much. I hope that encourages you to try to have faith.

> Come and hear, all you who have respect for God. Let me tell you what He has done for me. (Psalm 66:16 NIRV)

Steve Dugan
Mobile, Alabama
July 27, 2022

ACKNOWLEDGMENTS

Through the grace of God, some truly wonderful people have been very kind and helped us financially and in many other ways.

The people on this list were truly sent by God to save us. God sent them to rescue us when we were desperate and felt hopeless. Without their help, we would have been evicted from the home we were renting at the time, had our car repossessed or not had a car at all, not been able to afford medicine or medical or dental tests or treatment, not had food to eat, and not been able to survive for other reasons, too.

Without these people, I don't know how we would have made it through a marriage that has lasted almost fifty-two years at the time I am writing this. Unfortunately, I have forgotten many of the people who helped us, just like I have forgotten other important things about our lives.

Here is a list of the people I remember whose help has been so important to us.

Chip Barron

Lindsey Barron

Jack Brinkley

Joe Bullard

Jimmy Carter

Rosalynn Carter

Philip Chance

Shirley Clark

Ed Cole, III

Clarence Collins

Bobby Cremins

Carolyn Cremins

Bill Curry

Jan Davis

Dorsay Jones Eichorn

Gay Gillespie Faircloth

Jack Gaines

Day Gates

Audrey Henry

Jack Little

Buddy Luce

Sarah Louise Luce

Edward McDermott

Jim McKoon

Jane McLaughlin

Delano Palughi

Davis Pilot

Noel Robbins

Dottie Ryan

Bob Sherling

Tim Smith

Sally Stephens

Fred Stimpson

Sandy Stimpson

Roderick P. Stout

Nancy Dodd Tomlinson

Victor Tomlinson

William B. Turner

Claude Warren

John White-Spunner

Grace Woodford

Every name on this list and every name that I cannot remember which deserves to be on this list is itself a very important miracle that God did for us. These people will never know how grateful to God we are for them.

> You have come to Mount Zion and to the city of the living God, the heavenly Jerusalem, to an innumerable company of angels. (Hebrews 12:22 NKJV)

SPECIAL ACKNOWLEDGMENT

In closing, I acknowledge my Newnan High School friend, Diane Kabine Bagwell. I sent my story to many friends. Diane read it, edited it, and sent it back to me. After fifty years, she did not hesitate to invest her time and energy in this book.

It was Diane who pointed out the miracle of the poem as the turning point to the whole story. "It seems to me," she wrote, "that Julie's poem illustrated her love for you, even if she had not said it out loud." Diane's insightful observations were very meaningful to me.

One of the benefits of writing this book is being able to see important things that I had not understood before. God was faithfully working to bring Julie and me together, even when we did not realize the full significance of what He was doing.

It was God's plan to put Diane Kabine Bagwell back in my life after such a long time. I am grateful to her for pushing this book forward into the world.

> Not only so, but we also rejoice in our sufferings, because we know that suffering produces perseverance; perseverance, character; and character, hope. And hope does not put us to shame, because God's love has been poured out into our hearts through the Holy Spirit, who has been given to us. (Romans 5:3–5 NIV)

1 ANGELS UNAWARE

The story you will read in this book contains miracles God has done for me. It should give hope to everybody because I doubt anybody will read this book who is not a better person than I am.

After I lost all of our family's money in the 1990s, we went through some extremely difficult and stressful times. The first time we moved to Dauphin Island, Alabama in the late 1980s, we were millionaires. The second time we moved there, in the late 1990s, we were broke. Sometimes we didn't even have the money to buy food to eat.

But God sent two angels into our lives. They were a wonderful, Christian, African-American husband and wife from Prichard, Alabama. They came from Prichard to our house on Dauphin Island every week with a car trunk full of food for us. They had the best possible Christian spirit too.

In addition to bringing us boxes of groceries, they also brought us love and encouragement. They never wanted their acts of charity toward us to receive any recognition or attention. Most importantly, they never made us feel bad for needing charity. The smiles on their faces and their words of encouragement were so sincere that something important was unmistakable: they really loved us. I don't know how we would have made it through that time without their love. When they finished helping us, they went to Africa to be missionaries. I am describing them to represent all the people who helped us who I have somehow forgotten.

God did not do the miracles in this book for me because I was good. He did them because He is good. If God did these miracles for me, He will hear your prayers and care about them. Whether you are in prison on death row, in hospice care waiting to die, brokenhearted because a person you love doesn't love you, or watching your family suffer because of your sins and failures, it doesn't matter. No matter what you have done or how desperate of a situation you may have created for yourself and your family, God still loves you and hears your prayers, even if He does not grant them.

If you read this true book and come to the realization that God had a plan for my life, you must know that He has a plan for your life too. If you think He granted some of my prayer requests, you must believe He may grant some of yours too. If you recognize that God did miracles for me, you must have hope that He certainly may do some miracles for you too. He will grant your miracles if He thinks it is the right situation and if He thinks it is the right time to do them. Most of all, if you realize how much God loves me, you must understand that He loves you just as much.

> And now abideth faith, hope, charity, these three; but the greatest of these is charity. (1 Corinthians 13:13 KJV)

2 THE MIRACLE OF THIS BOOK

When I shared the first draft of *The Nine Words* with some of my friends, they thought it was powerful. But then they said things like, "Maybe you shouldn't use the real names of people. They might get mad." When I told my wife some text I included in the first draft, she said, "I don't feel good about you putting that in there." I understood how my friends and my wife felt. However, I thought that if I left out even the most personal details that happened or private people's names, the story would lose its power and credibility.

However, as it got nearer to the time to send the manuscript to the publisher, I concluded that I had been wrong. I decided the story was powerful enough without using the names of all the people involved and without sharing every personal detail about what happened. I feel good about that decision. A good book about God working miracles should not be embarrassing to anybody.

This is not a novel. It's just a story and a testimony. It is all true, to the best of my recollection.

When I tell it in person to people, they are very emotionally moved. However, it is very hard to make this story come across with 10 percent as much power when it is written down as when I can look people in the eyes and tell it to them in person. People who I tell this story to face to face can see and feel how sincere I am. They can hear the emotion in my voice. They see me unable to even speak at some points, and see my eyes water and tears come down my face at other points. People who can only read it will miss out on that. They will only have what is written on the pages of this book.

Think about "The Sermon on the Mount." It is powerful to read. Just imagine how powerful it must have been to the people sitting on the front row of the crowd. They were able to look into Jesus's eyes, see the expressions on His face, hear the emotion in His voice, and watch Him move His arms and hands when He said those words, which we now can only read over two thousand years later.

If you are one of the many good people who have difficulty believing anything that involves God or faith is true, I especially hope you will at least read this book. I feel like one of the main reasons God wanted it written is to show He did not quit doing miracles for people and even communicating with people one-on-one after He gave us the Bible all those hundreds of years ago. Who knows? Maybe He will speak to you for the first time in your life while you are reading this story.

I have not left out anything that I think God wants me to include. I would not do anything to take power or credibility away from this story. To be honest, there are a lot of things in this book about me that I am embarrassed about telling. But I must tell them. You need to know I am usually the opposite of a saint. In fact, I have not even been a sinner who managed to succeed at anything.

As I said before, God did not do the miracles in this book for me because I am good. He did them because He is good. The only reason I can think of to explain this is maybe He did the miracles in this story because He listened to my sincere prayers, and my prayers were consistent with His plan for my life.

In other words, since He did these miracles for me, He could do them for anybody. No matter how badly you have messed up, God loves you so much that He will hear your prayers and consider granting them.

Notice that I didn't say He *would* grant them. That is God's decision. I am not wise. I can't explain why God grants some prayers and refuses to grant others. All I can do is exactly what God told me to do: write this true story, try to get it published, and pray it helps somebody to not give up and to have faith.

If God uses this book to help just one single person anywhere in the world, it will be worth any embarrassment it causes me, my wife, or anybody else mentioned or described in this book.

I am only writing this because God told me to do it during the Christmas season of 2021. I was seventy-one years old. Because I had some noticeable and worsening symptoms of Parkinson's, with which I had been diagnosed over seven years before, I could no longer do the work I had been doing. This involved me going to court as a lawyer. I prayed and asked God what He wanted me to do. The answer I got was to write the story of *The Nine Words* and to try to get it published. Well, I have written it the best I can. Whether it will be published is up to God. If it is published, that will mean God will have done another big miracle.

The story is not about me, my wife, or the other people in the book. It is only about God. I hope it will encourage people to have faith in God and to understand that God listens to prayers and has a plan for every person's life. I know from experience it is very hard to believe those things, especially when you are going through a hard time, and you have prayed without receiving anything back from God. You will notice while reading that sometimes God answered the prayers in this book almost immediately, and sometimes He took years. I have also prayed for a lot of things He did not ever grant. However, those prayers were not related to *The Nine Words.*

You will also notice that on the biggest prayer in the book, I had to wait eight years for God to grant it. Before He did, He had to humble me by watching me try everything I could think of to achieve what I prayed for and finally completely give up on obtaining it. The minute I sincerely and utterly gave up, He immediately made it happen. I think He did it that way so I would have no doubt He, and not I, did it.

It is hard for me to make so much personal stuff about myself public. It's not something I wanted to do. I was so embarrassed about it that I prayed and asked God if I could make it less personal without sacrificing the ability of the story to help people. I also wondered if I could just write a fictional story like this story.

I decided I couldn't. This is a testimony. I know from being a lawyer that testimony has to be true to help anybody. I was also encouraged to tell the true story by reading scriptures. Here are some of them.

> I want you all to know about the miraculous signs and wonders the Most High God has performed for me. (Daniel 4:2 NLT)

> So do not be ashamed of the testimony about our Lord or of me his prisoner. Rather, join with me in suffering for the gospel, by the power of God." (2 Timothy 1:8 NIV)

> Many Samaritans from that town believed in Him because of the woman's testimony, "He told me all that I ever did." (John 4:39 ESV)

> As Jesus was getting into the boat, the man who had been demon possessed begged to go with him. But Jesus said, "No, go home to your family and tell them everything the Lord has done for you and how merciful He has been." (Mark 5:18–19 NLT)

3 THE MIRACLE OF THE NINE WORDS

It was in the fall of 1962 when this whole story started. I was twelve years old and in the seventh grade at Newnan Junior High School in Newnan, Georgia.

One of my two best friends, Ken Sharp, had invited my other best friend, Brad Sears, and me to spend the night with him. Late at night, we were upstairs in Ken's bedroom.

As boys almost always do, we started talking about girls. Ken was going steady with a girl named Julie Cole. He showed Brad and me a picture of her that she had given him, and what she had written on the back. The minute I saw that picture and saw her handwriting, I just knew she was the greatest girl in the world.

Julie was in the eighth grade. I know Ken, Brad, and I talked about her that night, but I don't remember anything that we said. I just know that seeing her face on that picture and seeing her handwriting made a very big impression on me.

A few weeks later that fall, right after school ended for the day, I was standing at the top of the steps of the Newnan Junior High School looking down at girls leaving school. The whole street in front of those steps was crowded with people getting into cars to go home.

I remember vividly seeing one girl, a very nice girl who I knew, standing in front of the car she was about to get into to ride home. I remember being able to see right through her. I could see right through her body to the car in front of which she was standing. Being able to do that struck me as very strange, because I knew that I had never been able to do that before. (I have never been able to do that since that day either.)

Then my eyes moved left to another pretty girl, who was standing in front of the car in which she was going to ride home. I could see right through her, too, just as I had been able to see right through the first girl. It is something I remember like it just happened today. I don't remember whether I knew that second girl or not.

Then, my eyes looked left from there to another girl standing in front of another car. I could not see through her. I remember thinking, *That girl is solid.* I was referring to her character. I knew she was a very different girl from all the others. She stood for something. That's what struck me so strongly. I also noticed she was very pretty. She looked just the way I wanted a girl to look.

Then, I heard a voice speak audibly into my ears. Somehow, I knew it was God. "That is a wise girl," the voice said. "You should marry her." Those nine words were the only words God ever audibly spoke to me. He never spoke to me before that day, and He has never spoken to me since that day either.

It made an incredibly strong impression on me. That night after supper, I went to bed early. I prayed for over two hours that one day God would let me marry that girl. I knew who she was from the picture Ken Sharp had shown me. That girl was Julie Cole.

That is the longest prayer I ever prayed in my life. I went into great detail with God. I remember asking him not to let her appearance change between then and when He let me marry her. I wanted her to look just the way she looked that day.

I didn't want anything about her to change. I didn't know her, but I sensed that she was good in every way.

I really can't remember anything else I said in that prayer. However, I looked at the clock after I finished the prayer. I know for sure that I had been praying for over two solid hours.

> And when the Lord saw that he turned aside to see, God called unto him out of the midst of the bush, and said, "Moses, Moses." And he said, "Here am I." (Exodus 3:4 KJV)

4 | FINDING MY PLACE

I never got over that day, and I never questioned or doubted what had happened. However, I didn't try to do anything about it for a long time either. I knew how special Julie was. It never dawned on me that she would ever want to spend time with me, at least not then.

I didn't dwell on her, but I never forgot what had happened. The next year I was in the eighth grade, and Julie was a freshman at Newnan High School. I didn't have a chance to see her, much less talk with her. I knew that she had broken up with Ken Sharp, but I never saw her.

The year after that, Julie was a sophomore at Newnan High, and I was a freshman. I didn't know it at the time, but that was the year Julie fell in love with a very nice young man; he was a senior and played on the basketball and baseball teams. He was very smart, popular, and handsome. Julie would be in love with him for the next five years.

I was very skinny and uncoordinated. In fact, I was so skinny that I was embarrassed to wear short sleeve shirts. At some point, I had gone out for football, basketball, and baseball, but I could never make any of the school teams.

I was so uncoordinated that the basketball coach cut me from the team after the first day of tryouts. After he did, he called me over, put his arm around my shoulder, and asked me if I had ever had polio. I said, "Not that I know of, Coach."

He said, "You would have known, kid."

I knew, at an early age, that I had to do something to compete with the athletes for girls. One day, I sat down at my desk in my room, as a nerd would do, and looked at a newspaper. I asked myself why girls liked athletes so much. I decided it must be because they were in the newspaper so often. I looked to see who else was in the newspaper on a regular basis.

There was an obituary section in the paper, but I figured it wouldn't help me with girls if I died. There was also a section about criminals. I figured it also wouldn't help me get girls if I were in prison. The only other people who seemed to be in the newspaper a lot were politicians. I decided to get involved in politics.

When there was a governor's election in Georgia in 1962, all the major candidates had a headquarters on the court square in downtown Newnan. I walked to the Carl Sanders headquarters and became a volunteer worker, doing anything I could. I liked working in politics, even though I was doing only the most mundane things, like putting bumper stickers on cars.

I also started my own little amateur newspaper, *The Nimmons Street Messenger.* The name of the paper changed to *The Newnan News* when our family moved from the house we were renting on Nimmons Street to another part of Newnan.

My parents decided to send me to the McCallie Academic Enrichment Camp in Chattanooga, Tennessee for eight weeks in the summer of 1964 because of my bad grades. I knew I couldn't keep writing my little newspaper while I was in Chattanooga. I asked Mrs. Thomason, whose family owned the local weekly paper *The Newnan Times-Herald* if I could write a weekly column during the time I was out of town at camp. She said I could.

My column was called "Hello, 'Dare." I guess the ramblings of a kid were unintentionally amusing to adults, because the column was popular enough that the paper let me keep writing it after I got home from camp.

That fall, when I started my freshman year at Newnan High, I got the idea of doing a radio call-in show. I went to see Mr. Jim Hardin, the owner and General Manager of WCOH, the local radio station. I asked him if I could start doing a call-in show for an hour on two or three nights a week. Amazingly, he had read my newspaper column and said I could do the radio show. We decided to call it "Party Line." A lot of young people liked to come to the station on the nights the show was broadcast live and participate in it. They thought it was a neat and fun thing to do.

It occurred to me that I finally might have done something that could interest Julie Cole. I had neither contacted her nor forgotten about her during the two years since God spoke those nine words to me.

I looked up her family's phone number and called her. She was very nice. I can still remember her voice during that call because it made the greatest possible impression on me.

It was a short call. I told her who I was and asked her if she wanted to come to the radio station for one of the broadcasts. She was polite and brief. She said, "No, thank you."

She sounded mature. But the chance to come to a radio

show broadcast, which appealed to many popular girls and boys I knew, did not have any appeal for Julie. The only good things about the call were that Julie did know who I was, and she was pleasant to me. I remember being excited to have talked to her, but sad that I wouldn't be seeing her.

That was during the 1964–1965 school year. At the end of that year, my momma, daddy, my sister, and I moved to Fort Valley, Georgia.

It was one hundred miles from Newnan. I would not see or talk with Julie again until my freshman year in college, which would be four years later. I never forgot about Julie and the nine words that God had spoken to me.

> "For I know the plans I have for you," declares the Lord, "plans to prosper you and not to harm you, plans to give you hope and a future." (Jeremiah 29:11 NIV)

5 | THE MIRACLE OF A SPECIAL FRIEND

That summer, after we moved to Fort Valley, I didn't know anybody or have any friends. There was a very nice girl in Newnan who knew how lonely I was. Out of the kindness of her heart, she sent me many letters that summer. I don't remember having known her very well in Newnan or how we started exchanging letters that summer, but her letters meant a lot to me.

On the days I got a letter from her, my day would feel special. I would write her a letter back. After supper, I would walk to the mailbox at the corner of our street and mail my letter to her. I still remember those walks to the mailbox at twilight every night, hoping that she would answer the letter I was about to mail. She was in Julie's class, but we never mentioned Julie in our letters.

Also during the summer, I went to see the owner of Fort Valley's weekly newspaper, Mr. Daniel K. Grahl. I asked him for a job. He said I could write all the articles I wanted to, and that he would pay me a penny per word for every article he published. I wrote a lot of articles.

At the end of the summer, school started. I still didn't know many kids. Early that fall, the high school held the annual Miss Vallihi beauty pageant at the high school auditorium on a Friday night. I walked the four or five blocks from our house to the high school and sat by myself. As I watched the pageant, one contestant stood out in my opinion. I thought she was extremely pretty, and I liked everything else about her, too.

I didn't know who she was until the master of ceremonies said her name on the stage. She was in the junior class—one year ahead of me.

I always felt like I was an uncoordinated guy with none of the qualities that girls found attractive. I knew that I needed a literal miracle from God to get to know such a special girl.

As I walked back home by myself after the pageant, I prayed about the situation. I said, "God, I really like that girl. I want you to make it possible for me to date her. And Lord, I don't want to rush You, but I want You to let me kiss her tomorrow afternoon. In Jesus's name, Amen." You may think it was silly, but that was literally my prayer, word for word.

This girl did not know I was alive, and I don't even remember if I knew exactly where she lived or how to get to her house. However, that next day after lunch, I walked to the end of our street, Hardeman Avenue. It had a dead end where the street stopped and the peach orchard began.

I walked into the peach orchard and came to a place where four paths intersected. I went right and kept walking. It finally came out in the back of an elementary school. I walked through the elementary school property to the street in front of the school. When I looked across the street, I saw a girl in her parents' garage working by herself on a float. It was the girl I had seen at the pageant the night before.

I went up to her, introduced myself, and said I would help her work on the float. I picked up a staple gun that was lying on the float and tried to help her staple crepe paper to the float. However, I accidentally stapled one of her fingers to the crepe paper. She went in her house. I stayed by the float. After a while, she came out with her finger bandaged.

I don't remember how this came about, but soon we walked through the front yard of the elementary school and around to the back. There was nobody else around. We sat down with our backs against a brick wall in a little area of the building with brick walls behind us and on both sides of us. The only thing in front of us was the peach orchard, which went on as far as I could see.

We hit it off, laughing and having a good time. Soon, we started kissing. While we were kissing, three guys from Fort Valley High School, who I didn't know yet, appeared. One of them was hitting his left palm with the fist he had made out of his right hand.

He said to her, "Are you all right?"

She looked up at them and said, "Yea, I'm fine, but thank you for checking on me." That just made the whole day even better, which was an almost impossible thing to do.

They left, and she and I went back to what we were doing. That is one of my favorite memories. It took a miracle for that to happen. God had granted the exact miracle that I had prayed for the night before.

At the end of the school year, this wonderful friend referred to some of these things in what she wrote on the last page of my yearbook, which I still have.

She wrote it in the spring of 1966, and I still read it every now and then. It still means a lot to me. When someone is as special to you as she was to me, you never forget him or her. I think about her often.

I failed to live up to what she thought I would become. I feel like I let her and my other friends at Fort Valley High School down. That is why I never went back for a school reunion.

Some people I have told this story to laugh when they hear about that miracle. I guess they think it's funny that God would grant a prayer that may not seem very important to most people. I tell them it's not funny. It was a very important miracle. The fact that God gave me a friendship with such a special girl gave me a lot of confidence and happiness.

Before Julie ever thought of dating me, this girl made me feel like I was an okay guy. That is worth more than all the money in the world. We never went steady, but we dated and were good friends as long as we were both in high school. We had a lot of happy times together, all because God heard a simple prayer.

> And Sarah said, "God hath made me to laugh, so that all that hear will laugh with me." (Genesis 21:6 KJV)

6 THE MIRACLE OF JIMMY CARTER

I kept working for politicians while I was at Fort Valley High. In early March of 1966, I helped organize an Affirmation Vietnam rally to show our support for our soldiers in that far away country. People filled the high school gym on a rainy Saturday night for the rally. I was the master of ceremonies, and the large crowd and patriotic theme attracted some politicians running for office in Georgia that year.

The school set aside a classroom where all the people on the program could gather and talk informally before the program started. In that little room, I met two wonderful men who would become my friends and for whom I would have the honor of working for many years to come.

I don't know what course my life would have taken if I hadn't met them. It turned out that working for one of them played an important role in my getting engaged to Julie four years later. Working for the other one was an important part of Julie's and my life together after we got married.

However, I had no idea of this on that night. In fact, my meeting these two politicians seemed about as unrelated to my dream of marrying Julie as anything could possibly have been. Nevertheless, as the Bible illustrates, people often do not understand what God is doing to allow them to fulfill His plan for their lives.

The first of these two politicians was Jack T. Brinkley. He was a member of the Georgia State House of Representatives from Columbus. He was thinking about running for the Democratic nomination for our district's recently vacated seat in Congress.

The second of these politicians that I met that night was State Senator Jimmy Carter of Plains. He was already actively campaigning for that open seat in Congress. We really hit it off great talking in that reception room before the rally began.

I introduced Carter to the crowd after the program began. He started his remarks by saying, "I just met Steve Dugan. He agreed to support me in my campaign this year, and I agreed to support him later on when he runs for President." The Fort Valley crowd got a big laugh out of that.

A few days after the rally, Jimmy Carter wrote me a letter. Fortunately, I still have it. He said that he enjoyed being at the rally, and that he would come to see me the next time he passed through Fort Valley. Not long after that, Jimmy Carter was passing through Fort Valley. He stopped at Fort Valley High School and asked the superintendent, Mr. Ernest Anderson, if he would get me out of class and let him use Mr. Anderson's office to talk with me.

Mr. Anderson was a very nice man and Carter had dedicated a lot of his work in the State Senate to educational matters. Someone came and got me out of my class.

When I walked into Mr. Anderson's office, there was Jimmy Carter. He closed the door and asked me to sit down. Then, he said, "I'm not running for Congress after all. I'm going to run for governor instead."

When I asked him why, he said, "Bo Callaway has decided to run for governor."

Bo Callaway had been running for the Republican nomination for our district's seat in Congress. He was an incredibly wealthy man for whose family beautiful Callaway Gardens was named.

Carter had been working to get the Democratic nomination for that seat and then beat Callaway in the general election in November. Carter was determined to represent the average citizens of Georgia, not just the wealthy.

I said, "I don't understand. Now that Callaway is running for governor, you would have a clear path to being elected to Congress. I thought that was what you wanted to do."

Jimmy Carter looked at me with his intense, determined eyes and said, "Nope. You don't understand. I want to beat Bo Callaway. Since he's running for governor, I'm going to run against him."

It was a strange thing to do, in my opinion. With Callaway out of the race for Congress, Jimmy Carter would have had a great chance to be elected to serve in the House of Representatives in Washington, D.C. On the other hand, there were already several Democrats running for the Democratic nomination for governor, and most of them were far better known and had much more campaign money than Carter.

Carter, however, had been the commander of a nuclear submarine. He was tough, hardworking, and extremely competitive. Callaway was a distinguished man, but Carter was going to run against him, no matter what Callaway ran for that year and no matter what the odds were against Carter winning.

What only God knew was that passing up a good chance to be elected to Congress and losing the election for governor in 1966 would set Jimmy Carter on the path to being elected president of the United States exactly ten years later.

I have often thought that the American people never got to see the real Jimmy Carter. He was very smart and even tougher. If he had shown the country that side of his personality while he was president, I believe he would have been re-elected to the White House in 1980.

In his campaign for the 1976 Democratic presidential nomination, he stressed the side of his personality that voters throughout America needed to see at that time in order for them to trust an unknown former southern governor to finish healing the country from Watergate. That side of his personality exemplified soft-spoken love for regular people, confidence in the goodness of the country, a true devotion to human rights, and sincere faith in God. I think that was the right approach for him to be nominated and elected in 1976. However, I also think that showing his tough, stern, and competitive side during the years he was president would have given him a better chance to be re-elected in 1980.

In 1966, Jimmy Carter came in third for the Democratic nomination for governor, and Jack Brinkley did get elected to

Congress. Both wonderful men played a huge role in my life for many years to come.

I don't think either Jimmy Carter or I would have believed it at the time, but not many years after I met Jimmy Carter at the Fort Valley High School gym he invited me to visit him at the White House.

> One who loves a pure heart and who speaks with grace will have the king for a friend. (Proverbs 22:11 NIV)

7 THE MIRACLE AT THE PEACH SHED

Like many other young people in Fort Valley, which is the county seat of Peach County, I started working that summer of 1966 at a peach packing shed. My job was to take shipping crates and fill them with fresh, just-picked peaches.

The shed was big. It had a tin roof, but no sides. There was no air conditioning or anything else. On some days, we kids were there from early in the morning until late at night. The worst things were the mosquito bites and the rash I got from being in contact with all that peach fuzz.

Between these two things and the oppressive heat, I was miserable and itching. One night, when it was particularly hot,

I prayed. I said, "God, I hate it here. It's driving me insane. Please help me."

You might think that praying to meet a beautiful girl and kiss her the next day and praying to be delivered from a peach shed are two silly things for which to pray. However, believe it or not, when I finished that prayer, somebody from the office of the peach shed walked up to me, tapped me on the shoulder, and said I had a phone call in the office. It was unusual for one of us kids to get a phone call at the peach shed, and this was the only phone call I ever got while I was working there.

I still remember how cool it felt when I walked into that little office, which was air conditioned. I picked up the phone, and this voice said, "Hello, Steve. This is Jimmy Carter. Would you like to come to work for me in my state headquarters in Atlanta this summer?"

I said, "Yes, sir. I sure would."

"Well," he said, "I'll talk with your parents and ask them if you can do it."

I still remember walking back to my place on the peach packing assembly line and wondering if this could really be happening. I didn't have to wait long to find out.

By the time I got home, Jimmy Carter had talked with Momma and Daddy. He told them that he would give me a room right next to his and Miss Rosalynn's in the Dinkler Plaza Hotel in downtown Atlanta, where his state campaign headquarters was located.

What he didn't tell them, and may not have realized himself, was that the Atlanta Playboy Club was on the other side of that room, which I would be sharing with Hamilton Jordan that summer. Boy, you talk about a change of scenery from that peach shed in Fort Valley!

He also promised Momma and Daddy that he would keep a constant eye on me. Momma and Daddy knew how much I loved politics, and they told him that I could do it.

The next Sunday afternoon, Daddy drove me to Atlanta and dropped me off with Carter's campaign manager, Mr. Bob Short. I want to give my parents a lot of credit for letting me do so many things like this.

God had granted another miracle answer to a prayer. Working that summer for Jimmy Carter was a great experience. I have many stories from that campaign, but I don't think they fit in with the main purpose of this book. I might write another one about my friendship with Jimmy Carter and his kindness to me.

I loved what I was doing but, in my eyes, God had still not done anything about granting my biggest and most fervent prayer: that I could marry Julie one day. What I could not have realized was that knowing Jimmy Carter and working for him would turn out to play a big part in God's plan for Julie and me to get married.

> And God heard the voice of the lad; and the angel of God called to Hagar out of heaven, and said unto her, "What aileth thee, Hagar? Fear not, for God hath heard the voice of the lad where he is." (Genesis 21:17 KJV)

8 MORE WORK IN POLITICS

During at least one of the next two summers, I worked for Congressman Jack Brinkley, who I had met at the same rally at which I met Jimmy Carter in 1966. Brinkley had been elected to the United States Congress that year.

He asked me to visit every high school in our thirteen-county district and organize Brinkley Advice Clubs. It was the same idea I had worked on in forming Teenagers for Carter during Carter's 1966 campaign for governor. The idea was to get young people interested in politics, just as I had, and build up a relationship between them and Congressman Brinkley. Like Carter, he really did care about what young people thought, and he was a very good politician.

Like Teenagers for Carter, the Brinkley Advice Clubs promoted good citizenship for the young people involved. They also influenced the parents of the young people who were members, because the parents were interested in what their children thought and discussed around the dinner table.

By doing this job, I was able to build a great friendship with Congressman Brinkley. Later on, after Julie and I were married and I finished my active-duty service in the Army, he gave me a job as his research assistant, working out of his district office in Warner Robins, Georgia. Several years later, he gave me the job of legislative assistant in Washington, D.C., but that is part of another story.

I enjoyed my job that summer organizing Brinkley Advice Clubs at high schools around the district, just as I enjoyed my work for Jimmy Carter. It kept me involved in politics. It also allowed me to meet a lot of smart and pretty girls, some of whom I was fortunate enough to date and whose friendships meant a lot to me. I have good news for all the nerds out there. That song is wrong. You don't have to be a football hero to get along with the beautiful girls. You can do it through politics, too!

I think God had a special reason for letting me become good friends with these great girls. He was not letting me get to know Julie yet. I don't think I would have been prepared to get to know Julie when I had the opportunity if I was not able to know these girls first. I think God has a purpose for and an interest in everything that happens in everybody's life. It's just not always easy to see it at the time.

I also stayed in close touch with Jimmy Carter. He had come from the bottom of the pack and almost made it into a runoff with former governor Ellis Arnall for the Democratic nomination for governor in 1966.

On August 15, 1967, he wrote me a letter looking back on his campaign of the previous year and telling me about his plans for the future. He said he mentioned me in speeches he was making around the state, and that he wanted me to work with him to get ready for the next campaign for governor, which was still three years away. I was honored that he cared about me and glad that he was including me in his future plans.

At the bottom of the letter was the notation "JC/rc," meaning Jimmy Carter had written it and Rosalynn Carter had typed it. Unlike the letters that Jimmy Carter had typed himself and sent to me, this one did not have any letters that had been typed over and it was well centered on the page. This is just an example of what a great team Jimmy and Rosalynn Carter were. Everything they did, they did together. Jimmy Carter could never have achieved any of the things he accomplished without Miss Rosalynn working with him. She was nice, but also tough and competitive.

After that, I started going to Plains and seeing Jimmy Carter from time to time. I remember going to his house during the Christmas holidays one year and several other visits to Plains, too. One time, I stayed at the house his mother lived in out in the country beside a little pond. Miss Lillian was a fun person to talk with. I also remember exchanging letters with him and Miss Rosalynn, who was always extremely kind to me.

I also got to know his three sons and became close friends with his youngest son, Jeff. Now, I have been able to talk with Jeff's son, Josh. How quickly life rushes by.

All these things were wonderful, but I still had no contact with Julie. I never felt like I wanted to marry anybody else. After all, God never said anything to me about any other girl.

All He ever said audibly to me was that day in 1962, when I saw Julie for the first time. I never forgot the nine words He spoke to me about her, "That is a wise girl. You should marry her."

I didn't think about Julie a lot during those days, because I was focused on what I was doing. However, every time I heard the word Julie, in person, on television, or in a movie, my mind went immediately to Julie Cole and those nine words God had spoken to me.

I never quit knowing how special she was, even though I had only heard her say three words to me in my whole life: "No, thank you."

During the summer of 1968, the man who had beaten Jimmy Carter in the 1966 election and become governor of Georgia wanted to include some young people in Georgia's delegation to the Democratic National Convention in Chicago. When he asked Jimmy Carter for some recommendations, Carter suggested me. The governor called my daddy and asked him if I could be a delegate. Daddy said I could.

At eighteen, I was having a wonderful time in politics. However, none of what I was doing could even get Julie's attention. She was in love with her long-time boyfriend, and my name never even crossed her mind.

At a time like that, there was no reason to think God was going to grant my prayer that I be able to marry Julie one day— except for one thing. God had told me that I should marry her. Why would God say that, if He wasn't going to somehow, someday give me the chance to do it?

As you know, we count as blessed those who have persevered. You have heard of Job's perseverance and have seen what the Lord finally brought about. The Lord is full of compassion and mercy. (James 5:11 NIV)

9 | THE MIRACLE AT THE AIRPORT

After I returned from the convention in Chicago, it was time for me to leave for my freshman year at Washington and Lee University in Lexington, Virginia. I was getting much farther away from the chance of seeing Julie. Had I just imagined those nine words? There was no sign that God was going to grant my biggest prayer.

As soon as I arrived at Washington and Lee in August of 1968, I became homesick. Nevertheless, I did the best I could to make it work. I was there, and it was too late for me to change my mind about where to go to college.

At that sad time, I could not see how God was going to use this unlikely place so far from Georgia to bring me into contact with Julie. Miraculously, He did.

There was another student at Washington and Lee named Matt Cole. He was from Newnan, and his family lived just one house down from Julie's family on Woodbine Drive in Newnan. He and Julie had the same last name, but they weren't related. However, their families were close friends.

When it came time for Christmas vacation, Matt Cole and I took the same flight from Roanoke, Virginia back to Atlanta. When the plane landed in Atlanta and I walked to the baggage claim area of the airport, I saw Julie. I immediately recognized her, even though I had not seen or talked with her since that day four years before.

Julie was sitting there with Matt Cole's mother, waiting for Matt and his baggage to arrive. I said, "Hello" as I approached where she was sitting. I can still see her. She looked pretty and mature, just like I would want a girl to look.

I did not think she would even know who I was, and I was surprised when she said, "Hello, Steve." I can still hear her saying those words. I didn't say anything else. I just couldn't believe that Julie Cole knew who I was.

I thought she was a nice young woman who was being polite. However, it meant so much to me that she recognized me, knew my name, and spoke to me. I have never forgotten that moment.

It turned out that Julie had broken up with her boyfriend that fall. I didn't know anything about that at the time.

But those who hope in the Lord will renew their strength. They will soar on wings like eagles; they will run and not grow weary; they will walk and not be faint. (Isaiah 40:31 NIV)

10 | THE MIRACLE OF OUR FIRST DATE

During my entire life, my parents had never been to even one single musical concert. For some reason, while I was at home during that holiday season, they went to one on a Sunday afternoon at Mercer University in Macon, Georgia, less than an hour from Fort Valley.

The next morning, my mother said, "Guess who we saw at the concert yesterday? Julie Cole and her mother. You should call her and ask her for a date."

I said, "Momma, Julie Cole doesn't want to go out with me." A few minutes later, however, I called her. I don't even remember how I got her number. She answered. I asked her if she wanted to eat supper and go to a movie that night. She said she would.

I had never forgotten the nine words that God had told me about Julie. I didn't know much, but I did know that she was the girl I wanted to marry. I had not thought about her much since our family moved away from Newnan four years before, but I hadn't forgotten or doubted the nine words that God had spoken to me back then either.

That night, when I picked her up and we got in the car, the first thing I remember doing was, incredibly, telling her that I loved her and asking her to marry me. She says she thought that I was a nice and sincere boy, but that I surely didn't make her want to marry me.

Nonetheless, I was determined not to waste this opportunity to be with Julie for which I had waited so long. I spent much of the rest of the date just driving around, repeating how much I loved her, and trying to convince her to marry me. I think we also went to the Macon Drive-In and saw *Finian's Rainbow*, starring Fred Astaire and Petula Clark. She later told me that, when she got back to the dorm room where she was staying, she told her friends that she was starving. Because I had been so intensely focused on telling her how much I loved her and trying to get her to marry me, I had forgotten to take her to dinner.

When I took Julie back to her dormitory at Mercer, I walked

her to the door. I remember this like it was yesterday. Before we got to the door, I said, "Could I kiss you good night?"

She said, "If you want to." It was our first kiss. I remember it. It sure was special for me. She later said it was a good kiss.

Well, that set my course. From that point on, I thought about her all the time. Soon, my Christmas vacation was over, and it was time for me to take the flight back from Atlanta to Roanoke and return to far off Lexington, Virginia.

I remember spending the whole trip back wishing I could be with Julie and trying to figure out a way to get her to love me and marry me. There was no doubt about what I wanted to do. I was in love with her. However, I sure needed God to perform a huge miracle to make her want to marry me.

> But if we hope for what we do not yet have, we
> wait for it patiently. (Romans 8:25 NIV)

II | THE MIRACLE OF THE LUCKY BREAK

I don't remember what happened between us for the rest of that school year or during the summer of 1969. I don't remember if I saw or communicated with Julie at all. I think I must have, but I just don't remember.

I may have spent the summer of 1969 working at the Blue Bird Bus Company in Fort Valley, where my daddy was the financial director. I know I worked there one full summer and part of another one.

The only thing I can find related to that summer is a letter from Jimmy Carter dated July 7, 1969. In it, he invited me to a meeting on Saturday, July 19, 1969. He wrote that the purpose of the meeting was to discuss his candidacy and campaign plans. He was making final plans to run for governor again the next year.

I feel sure that I went to that meeting, but I just can't remember anything about it. It is sad to get old and forget entire years of your life. That's why I wish so much that I had kept a journal. Just writing two or three sentences a day would have been more than enough to remind me of everything that happened. However, when you're young and interesting things are happening, you don't believe you'll ever forget them. Now, the memories from those times are sadly lost forever.

I hope somebody will contact me and tell me they remember doing something with me back then. It would mean a lot to me to find out something I did during that time.

When the summer of 1969 ended, it was time for me to go back to Washington and Lee. The afternoon before I was supposed to leave home, I heard the back doorbell ring. When I answered the door, a man from the local Chevrolet dealership handed me some keys and said, "This is your new car." I couldn't believe it. There, in the garage, was a beautiful, brand-new Chevrolet Malibu, in the white and gold colors of my favorite team, Georgia Tech. I don't remember how I had thought I was going to get back to Washington and Lee. However, I do remember being happily surprised to see that car, which my parents had bought for me.

I would have never believed that in just one year and a few weeks, Julie and I would be married. That same car would be our first car, in which we would have many wonderful times together.

The plan was for me to drive for about five hours the next day to Clinton, South Carolina and spend the night with my beloved Aunt Ruth and Uncle Lykes Henderson and some of my cousins. One of them, Lewis, was one of the best friends I ever had, and he would be an usher at our wedding.

As planned, I got to Clinton late the next afternoon. After I arrived, Lewis and I decided to throw a football in their big front yard. I caught a pass and tripped on the curb of the driveway. When I fell, I was in a lot of pain, but Lewis thought I was joking and went inside. Finally, somebody came out and saw I was not joking. The person helped me into the den and put me in a lounge chair, so my foot could be supported. I remember watching *The F.B.I.* with Aunt Ruth and Uncle Lykes.

When my ankle started to swell, Aunt Ruth said she would take me to the doctor the next morning if my foot was not better. The next morning, my left ankle had swollen to the size of a grapefruit. When Aunt Ruth took me to the doctor, he said I had broken it and put a cast on it that went up to my knee.

Lexington, Virginia is a hilly town and is covered with ice and snow for much of the winter. In addition, I was planning to live in the attic of a lady's house. It was decided that I wouldn't be able to get around, if I tried to go to Washington and Lee for the first half of that school year. Therefore, I went back to Fort Valley and became a transient student at Mercer University in Macon.

Julie had transferred from Mercer to LaGrange College in LaGrange, Georgia. Fortunately, LaGrange was only about two hours from Macon. When I called her and asked for a date, Julie agreed to come from LaGrange to Macon and stay with some friends of hers in her old dorm.

I don't remember much about the dates that Julie and I had that fall. I think we may have gone to the little theatre in Macon on one of them to see a performance of *The Music Man*.

The next thing I specifically remember was going to Newnan to have a date with Julie a few days before Christmas. I was excited that she would have dates with me. While she was friendly to me, I was not making any progress on trying to get her to fall in love with me. At least I was spending time with her, so I was happy and excited and hoped she would start to feel more for me than just friendship.

When I recently asked her what she thought of me back in those days, Julie said she remembered that I talked a lot, cared about her, and that she felt comfortable around me. However, there was nothing more than friendship on her part.

Looking back on it, I think making her feel cared about and comfortable with me was probably a good thing, especially since she had recently broken up with a very nice guy with whom she had been in love for five years.

Soon, Christmas vacation was over. It was the start of 1970, and time for me to go back to Washington and Lee again. My time as a transient student at Mercer in Macon was over.

However, I have always thought of my ankle injury that fall on my way to Washington and Lee as my lucky break because it opened the way for me to spend more time with Julie. However, it really wasn't a lucky break. It was a miracle. It was part of God's plan to get Julie and me married.

> The Lord upholds all who fall and lifts up all who
> are bowed down. (Psalm 145:14 NIV)

12 | HOPE AND HEARTBREAK

Early that spring, I asked Julie if I could come spend a weekend with her and her momma and daddy in Newnan. She said that I could. I had never gone for a weekend visit to a girl's house before, so I hoped this meant she was beginning to love me.

When I got up on the morning I was going to drive to Newnan, I noticed there was a pimple on the tip of my nose. I stopped at the drug store in Lexington and bought a bag of cotton balls and a bottle of rubbing alcohol.

I rubbed alcohol on that pimple the whole seven hours I drove from Lexington, Virginia to Newnan, Georgia. By the time I got to Julie's house, that pimple had grown so much and gotten so shiny that I looked like Rudolph the red-nosed reindeer. I was so embarrassed. It was only later that I found out that pimples feed on rubbing alcohol.

When I knocked on her parents' front door and her father opened it, I tried to cover my nose with my left hand and shake his hand with my right hand. What a terrible time to have spent seven hours growing a gigantic pimple. Nevertheless, Julie and her momma and daddy were extremely nice to me.

Julie and I sat in her living room and talked that Friday night. On Saturday afternoon, Julie's mother took Julie and me to visit a beautiful estate outside of Newnan.

On Sunday, Julie and I went to her church, the Central Baptist Church. I remember giving her a note in church saying emphatically that I loved her and wanted to marry her.

After lunch, it was time for me to start the long drive back to Washington and Lee. Julie walked with me down the steps that went from the main floor of her house to the basement, which had a door into the garage.

When we said goodbye, I kissed her several times. However, the visit ended on a crushing note. She said, "I'm never going to love you. I'm falling in love with somebody else."

I was so sad. I didn't know what to say. I got in my car and drove out of her driveway. She told me after we got married that she hadn't been falling in love with anybody else. She just didn't feel like she would ever love me. She thought the best way to keep me from getting even more hurt was to tell me what she said, so I wouldn't get my hopes up. She was trying to protect my feelings, not hurt me.

It hurt so badly. I cried all the way to the halfway point of the drive back, which was Charlotte, North Carolina. It was about 9:00 p.m. I decided I did not want to go back to Washington and Lee. I was completely devastated. The girl I had wanted to marry since I was twelve years old had just told me that my dream was never going to come true. My life seemed pointless and painful.

I stopped in Charlotte and called Jimmy Carter at his home in Plains. He had already decided to run for governor that year, and I had agreed to work for him out of his campaign headquarters in Atlanta that summer. I told him the whole story. He was very nice. He said I could quit Washington and Lee, come live at his house in Plains, and start working for him in his campaign right then. That made me quit crying. I told him I would do it. As I drove from Charlotte the rest of the way to Lexington, Virginia, I first prayed. Then, I decided that I would not give up on getting Julie to marry me.

I got back to Washington and Lee after midnight. The next day, I called my parents and told them I was going to quit

Washington and Lee and go to Plains to live with and work for Jimmy Carter. They were flabbergasted.

My sister Sally called me and said it would break Momma and Daddy's heart if I dropped out of Washington and Lee. I agreed to stay. I called Jimmy Carter and told him I would not be coming to live with his family, but that I would report to his headquarters in Atlanta and begin working for him as soon as the school year ended at Washington and Lee.

> The sacrifices of God are a broken spirit; a broken
> and contrite heart, O God, you will not despise.
> (Psalm 51:17 ESV)

13 | THE MIRACLE OF THE POEM

For the rest of the school year at Washington and Lee, I did not see Julie. However, she demonstrated the kind of person she was by continuing to care about me and by exchanging letters with me. I decided that I had been appearing way too anxious to have her love me, so I decided to try playing it cool.

My plan to do this was to quit writing her back the day I got a letter from her. Whenever I got a letter from her, I would roll two dice and combine them to get a number from two to twelve. Then I would force myself to wait that many days before I wrote her back.

It was a stupid plan, but that's what I did. Fortunately for me, I rolled a lot of low numbers. I don't think I could have waited twelve days to answer one of Julie's letters.

I wish so much that I still had the letters she wrote to me. However, over the intervening years, they have been lost. The most memorable one was the one she wrote me for my birthday, May 19. I didn't even know that Julie knew my birthday, but she did.

She sent me a very nice card and a wonderful poem she had written for me. I had been adopted, when I was a little baby. I didn't like to think about it or talk about it, because I knew my adoptive parents were my true Momma and Daddy, who God had intended to be my parents. They had wanted me, loved me, and sacrificed for me my whole life, and I thought it would be disloyal to them to even think or talk about my biological parents, who had abandoned me.

I must have talked about it to Julie, because she wrote me the most beautiful poem for my birthday. I wish I had it or remembered it, but I don't. I do, however, remember how it started: "Today, some sad mother sits and cries."

She was telling me in her poem that my biological mother was thinking about me on my birthday and crying because she had never gotten to know me. That was so powerful and moving to me. Nobody else had ever been wise enough to understand how much I needed to hear that. It made me cry. It still makes me cry whenever I try to tell someone about it.

While I was writing this story, I was visiting with my friend Fred Stimpson of Mobile, Alabama to discuss this book. I told him the entire story. When I got to the part about Julie writing me that poem, I could not get the words of the first line out of my mouth. I tried, but I couldn't. We were sitting alone at a big conference room table in a room across from his office. When I couldn't get the words out, I got out of my chair, looked at Fred, and tried again. For some reason, I thought that I might be able to do it if I were standing up instead of sitting down.

I still couldn't get the words out. I just looked at him and froze. He could tell how emotional this subject and Julie's poem were to me. My eyes got all wet, and then a few tears started flowing down my cheeks. Finally, I regained some composure and was able to get the words out in a cracking voice. It was an emotional experience for both Fred and me.

All my life, I have had a terrible fear of abandonment and a sense of insecurity. When I wake up in the morning, I feel like I must prove myself from scratch to everybody I meet, no matter who they are.

I never thought that, just because somebody liked me the day before or even for every day for ten years before, that he or she would still like me the next time I saw him or her. I thought I had to earn a person's friendship and approval every day.

It is a heavy burden to live that way, and people I know don't like it. They think I'm either unnecessarily taking up their time by repeating myself or being insincere. I'm not. I'm desperate for people to like me, but I have a hard time believing they do. I think that's why I've always liked girls to whom I was attracted so much. My relationships with girls I really liked were the only relationships that assured me the other person really, truly did like me. It was the only kind of human communication that I ever really trusted.

I believe that all of this was because I thought my biological parents had not wanted to keep me. In my heart, I took that to mean I must be a horrible person, that they knew something about me that was so bad that they didn't want me.

It was hard for me to believe in unconditional love, even from God. It caused me stress, anxiety, depression, and fear all my life.

My adoption was a subject that I would not talk about with anyone, because I thought it would be disloyal to Momma and Daddy for me to do so. I went to psychiatrists, psychologists, and counselors about my symptoms, but I would never talk about the issue of my adoption. Some of them asked if they could hypnotize me to find out what was causing my problems.

I would not let them. I was afraid something about my biological parents would come up, and I thought it would be disloyal to Momma and Daddy for me to talk about them. I just would not talk about it, and I don't remember any of these people asking me much about it.

Somehow, Julie figured out the whole problem and wrote me that moving poem to address it. Until then, it had never crossed my mind that my biological mother might think about me on my birthday. That poem was, and still is, stunningly powerful to me.

Another thing contributed to my fear of abandonment, insecurity, and inability to believe in unconditional love. When I was four years old, Momma and Daddy decided to adopt a little girl. Because they didn't want me to feel threatened by this, they took me with them to the orphanage. The three of us were sitting in a room. The lady in charge came in, and someone brought in three little bassinets in three pastel colors.

There was a little baby girl in each one. Somebody said, "Stevie, go pick your sister." I think they wanted me to feel included in what was happening.

I walked across the room and looked down at those three little babies. I was horrified by the whole situation. I picked the baby in the middle bassinette. Somebody said, "That's your new sister, Sally."

I remember so well that, as we were leaving that room, the lady who had been in charge said, "Well, if this little girl doesn't work out, just bring her back and we'll give you another one." Maybe the lady was just joking. I don't know. What I do know is that I got the indelible impression that since I was adopted too, I could also be returned, if I didn't "work out."

My wonderful momma and daddy never did anything to make me think that was the case. Nevertheless, the impression had found its way into my mind and, since I was embarrassed to talk about it with Momma and Daddy, it stayed there.

The wonderful poem Julie wrote me made me think about these disturbing memories. It also showed me something else. Julie had said a month or six weeks before that she could never love me. However, that she put so much thought into that poem for my birthday made me realize she did care about me. That meant a lot to me.

She didn't sign the card or the poem "Love, Julie." Instead, she wrote, "Sincerely, Julie" on both. My immediate reaction was that she was sincere about being my friend and caring about me but was still sure she would never be able to love me. I was happy and heartbroken all at the same time.

It also reminded me of the nine words that God had spoken to me about Julie. God had said, "That is a wise girl. You should marry her." God was right when He told me she was wise, but why had He told me that I should marry her when she had told me she could never love me?

I wondered what was so wrong with me that my biological parents didn't want me, and the girl I loved said she could never love me. What was so bad about me? Could I do anything to make myself worthy of being loved?

Of course, that was just how I felt. As Julie's poem showed, I really didn't know how my biological mother felt about me, and I needed to appreciate the great love she showed by giving birth to me. My high school friend, Diane Kabine Bagwell, told me she thought that Julie's poem was the turning point of the whole story. Diane said it was thoughtful and showed that Julie was beginning to love me, even if she didn't say it. God was already drawing Julie and me towards getting married, even though I did not realize it or fully understand it at that time.

> So do not throw away your confidence; It will be richly rewarded. You need to persevere so that when you have done the will of God, you will receive what He has promised. (Hebrews 10:35–36 NIV)

14 | THE MIRACLE WEEK

When the school year ended, I went home and then went to Atlanta to spend the summer working out of Jimmy Carter's campaign headquarters. During the first part of June, I gave up on Julie ever falling in love with me.

However, I wanted to tell her good-bye in person. I called her and asked her if I could come see her at her parents' house in Newnan that night. She said I could.

I didn't even plan on going inside her house. I thought she would be glad that I wasn't going to be bothering her anymore, especially since she had told me she was falling in love with somebody else.

On that fateful night, which I believe was Monday, June

15, 1970, I drove to Newnan and knocked on the door. Julie answered it.

I said, "Well, I've got some great news for you. I give up. I've been trying to get you to love me for about a year and a half, and all I've succeeded at doing is bothering you and making myself miserable. So I've come to tell you good-bye. I hope you have a great life."

I reached out my hand to shake her hand and leave. You have to understand that this wasn't a ploy. This was sincere. I had tried, I had failed, I had finally accepted that Julie was never going to fall in love with me, and I had given up.

I really thought Julie would just say, "Thank you," and walk back into her house. When I looked in her eyes, I saw something I had never seen before. For the first time since I had known her, she looked mad. I thought, "That is a good sign." Then, she asked me in.

We sat on the sofa in her parents' living room for about four hours. I asked her if I could come back the next night, Tuesday, and she said I could.

The only other thing I really remember about that Monday night was that there was a record player in the room and a Barbara Streisand record. We listened to it over and over all night long. Every time it came to the upbeat song, "Secondhand

Rose," I would get up off the sofa and dance around that room, because I was so happy to be unexpectedly spending time with Julie. I still love that song.

Tuesday night when I knocked on the door, Julie answered it and gave me a tin of cookies. She said she had made them for me that day. Well, that was a big deal to me, because the only other time any girl had cooked me anything was on my birthday in 1967, when Kaye Cooper made me a cherry pie and brought it to my house. I'll always remember and appreciate that, too.

We sat down on the same sofa as the night before. We listened to the same record repeatedly. Sometime that night, I told Julie again that I loved her. Only this time, praise God, she said, "I love you, too."

I was so happy that I didn't know what to do. How could everything change so much in twenty-four hours? I still don't know the answer to that. I asked her if I could come back the next night, and she said I could.

When I got there on Wednesday night, we sat on the same sofa and listened to the same record again. Sometime that night, I asked her again if she would marry me. This time she said, "Yes."

Well, this happened almost fifty-two years ago, and it's sort of a blur. I wish I had kept a diary, because that's all I remember, except that I asked her if I could come back the next night, and she said I could.

The next night was Thursday. The only thing I remember about that night is that we went in Julie's momma and daddy's den and told them we were engaged. I was nervous and scared. This was something I had never done before. I was afraid her daddy would get mad and ask me a lot of reasonable questions that I wouldn't be able to answer.

However, Julie's momma and daddy were as nice and calm as they could be. The only other thing I remember from that night is that Julie and I planned to drive to Fort Valley the next night, a Friday, and tell my momma and daddy.

I didn't give Momma and Daddy any advance notice because I wanted to surprise them. I thought they would be thrilled that Julie had agreed to marry me.

On Friday night, I picked Julie up and we drove the one-and-a-half-hours to Fort Valley. Momma and Daddy knew that I was coming home for the weekend, but they weren't expecting me to bring anybody with me.

When we got to Momma and Daddy's house, we all sat down in the den. I then told Momma and Daddy that Julie and I were engaged. I got an unexpected reaction. Daddy used a phrase I had never heard him say before. It had to do with how unprepared he thought I was to get married.

Momma and Daddy were wild about Julie. That wasn't the problem. The problem was that Daddy didn't think that I was in any way ready to get married and take care of a wife. Soon, everybody was happy with our plans. Julie stayed in the guest room, which was right next to my room upstairs.

I don't remember anything else about that weekend but, when it was over, our lives had been miraculously changed by God in just one week. On Sunday, I drove Julie back to Newnan and went back to Jimmy Carter's headquarters in Atlanta to work.

> Then shall the young women rejoice in the dance, and the young men and the old shall be merry. I will turn their mourning into joy; I will comfort them and give them gladness for sorrow. (Jeremiah 31:13 ESV)

15 | THE TRIP

Julie's daddy had already paid for her to take a trip with a group led by the president of LaGrange College to the Far East from June 22 through July 16. I had forgotten all these exact dates, but I discovered them from reading some letters I wrote Julie while she was on her trip. Incredibly, that means we became engaged one week, and she left for Japan on Tuesday morning of the following week.

It also makes me realize that God's hand had to be all over this. If, instead of calling her the Monday I did, I had waited and called her the next Monday, she would not have been able to have that date with me because she was leaving the next morning on her trip. The Miracle Week would have never happened, at least not then.

I hated that she was going to be gone. However, she said her daddy had paid for the trip, and that he wouldn't be able to get his money back if she didn't go. Plus, it was a once in a lifetime opportunity for her.

Much of the time she was gone, I was driving around rural Georgia to talk to people on behalf of Jimmy Carter. One afternoon, I was driving through a pine tree covered part of the state near the South Carolina border. I was listening to the car radio, as I almost always did. I was thinking about Julie and missing her when a song I had never heard before came on the radio. It was Bobby Sherman singing his 1970 hit record "Julie, Do Ya' Love Me."

It sure did ask the question that was on my mind. We had gone from good-bye to engaged in one week, and then back to good-bye again. Now she was halfway around the world with plenty of time to rethink her decision. Would she change her mind? I was worried.

I wrote her at least one letter every day. She gave me the addresses for every place she would be on her trip and the days she would arrive at each place. I would mail the letters to the place she would be five days after I mailed them.

No matter where she was, the first two lines of the address

would be "Miss Julie Cole, c/o Dr. W. G. Henry Group." She wrote me at my parents' address in Fort Valley.

I went to see the postmaster in Fort Valley. Since I was traveling around the state for Jimmy Carter, I asked him how I could get her letters the quickest when I was near Fort Valley. He told me to just come to the back of the Post Office and knock on the door. He said he would keep them and give them to me any time I came by. I really appreciated that. There were many early mornings when I knocked on that door and he brought me a packet of letters from Julie with a big smile on his face.

Unfortunately, I somehow lost the letters that Julie sent me. I can still see them, but I just lost them. Oh, how I wish I still had them. I also remember that she was so thoughtful that she wrote letters to Momma and Daddy and Sally while she was gone, too.

We do have the letters I wrote to Julie while she was on her trip. On July 8, 1970, Julie turned 21 years old in Taipei, Taiwan. I wrote the following letter to her there

Wednesday July 1, 1970

Dear Julie,

Well, if my calculations are right, (which they probably aren't), you should be getting this on your birthday. I wish you a very happy one and I am very happy that we will be celebrating the rest of our birthdays together. Remember, we will have a little birthday party for you as soon as you get back.

The campaign is going better now than it was. Today I am going to be in Elberton and three other towns. Yesterday I was in Lincolnton and Washington, and it was very encouraging to hear so many folks say they liked Carter. I feel like Carter has an excellent chance to win. I understand he spoke in Newnan last Monday afternoon.

I am sorry I have no news to write you, but while I'm living on the road like this, I know no news myself. I do know one thing, however: our relationship is making me a better person. Since becoming engaged to you, I have become more concerned with everything and everybody around me. I work harder now than before, because our life together has given me a great new incentive to do my best. My disposition has improved, because the sense of happiness and thankfulness I feel as a result of our friendship cannot help but spill over into my association with other people. The feeling of frustration which used to cause me to view the whole world as against me has given away to a sense of assurance which causes me to see everything as part of God's great plan. I believe that God brought us together, and I believe that I have never felt closer to Him than I do now when I have the love he has given us to share.

In my heart, I believe that no two people ever had any more to be thankful for than we do. I love you, and this love we share has made me both happier and better. Because of our love, I see more clearly than ever before how dependent we all are on God and how independent all true happiness is from the material world. Together with you, I believe we can go through our life together serving God by loving each other and helping our world.

I have a gift I will give you for your birthday when you return. In the meantime, let me give you the knowledge that I know whatever I turn out to be—President, Governor, Lawyer, Preacher, salesman, janitor, etc.—I will be a better person because God has given us each other.

I love you.
StDugan

I have copied that letter word for word. I have not changed any grammar or spelling. I have not omitted or added anything, no matter how pompous or embarrassing it now seems to me.

Looking at what I wrote, I can see that I was very immature, insecure, full of myself, and verbose. It is embarrassing in many ways. Nevertheless, I put it in here for one reason. It shows that even back then, when we had just gotten engaged, I knew that this wonderful thing was only happening because of the intervention of God.

I may have been a fool and gotten most everything else wrong, but I got that right. While it has not made me a successful person or a good husband, it is only because of that same grace of God that I am typing this almost fifty-two years later and am still married to the same wonderful girl.

For most of the time Julie was on her trip, I would go to see a movie at night with some of the other young people working for Jimmy Carter or go to a Braves game with them when I was in Atlanta. I remember seeing two movies I really liked: *Patton* and *Darling Lili*. I also remember one I didn't like: *Chisum* starring John Wayne. I am a big John Wayne fan, but I thought that was a horrible movie. Maybe I was getting sick of going to movies with a bunch of guys from the campaign and wanted Julie to hurry up and get back.

On the night of Tuesday, July 14, 1970, I was sitting with Momma and Daddy in their den in Fort Valley watching the baseball all-star game on TV. The phone rang. It was Julie calling from Honolulu, Hawaii. It was the first time I had heard her voice since she had been gone. Back then, long distance phone calls were a big deal. People like us usually only made one when there was an emergency or to our relatives on Christmas day.

Julie later told me that she had to pay for that call with her own money right after we finished talking. She said that, after paying for it, she had less than one dollar left.

It made me so happy that Julie had called. She said they had flown from Japan to Honolulu that day and they would get back to Atlanta on Thursday morning at 9:30 a.m., about thirty-six hours later.

It was dark outside in Fort Valley when Julie called, but it was still daylight in Hawaii. Julie said their hotel was right on the famous beach at Waikiki. She said she had just come back from a swim in the ocean.

On Thursday morning, July 16, 1970, I went to the Atlanta airport to pick Julie up. When her plane landed, I watched the people getting off. There she was with an older man, who I figured must be the president of her college.

I had written her so many letters addressed to "Miss Julie Cole, c/o Dr. W. G. Henry Group," and I was so excited to see Julie, that I reached out my hand to the man and said, "Hello, you must be Dr. Group." Everybody started laughing, because his name was Dr. Henry. He had just been leading the group of which Julie had been part.

At any rate, Julie was home, and I was extremely happy. That was July 16, 1970. Julie and I had no idea that in two months and three days, we would be married.

> Trust in the Lord with all thine heart; and lean not unto thine own understanding. In all thy ways acknowledge Him, and He shall direct thy paths. (Proverbs 3:5–6 KJV)

16 | SPECIAL SUMMER

In preparing this book, I read all the letters that I wrote to Julie on that trip for the first time since I wrote them almost fifty-two years before.

The letters I wrote to Julie were pathetic. They reeked of immaturity and insecurity. In reading them, it seems like I was afraid that she would change her mind about marrying me while she was on that long trip.

However, things had happened so quickly. On June 15, I went to her house, told her that I had given up on her ever loving me, and told her good-bye forever. Then, everything changed.

In one day, we said we loved each other. In two days, we

were engaged. In three days, we told her parents. In four days, we told my parents. Four days after that, she left on a twenty-four-day trip to the other side of the world. I guess I was just sort of in shock.

Julie has always been strong, quiet, humble and mature. In her senior yearbook at Newnan High School, the editors included a large picture of her. Under the picture, they put the three words Julie's classmates thought described her best. Those words were, "Serene, Responsible, Truthful."

Well, they certainly were right. Julie is and always has been all those things, and they are all indicative of the nine words that God told me when I was twelve years old in 1962: "That is a wise girl. You should marry her." Those qualities are consistent with being wise.

Unfortunately, I am much the opposite of serene. There are also many times when I have been irresponsible. I have also not always been truthful. In addition, I am immature and insecure.

I was also conceited, until I was humbled by my horrible sins, foolish decisions, crushing failures, numerous mistakes, and terrible temper. I will never understand why a person who has the qualities that Julie has would have decided to marry me.

Therefore, it is no wonder that I was worried she would

rethink everything and change her mind about marrying me on that trip. However, despite my immature letters, she didn't. How I wish I had the letters she wrote me, so I could see what she was thinking. I ask her about stuff like that even today, but my questions seem to irritate her, and she just says she can't remember.

At any rate, when she got back on July 16, the plan was that Julie would go back for her senior year at LaGrange College that fall, and that we would get married during the summer of 1971. On a Sunday in mid-August, we loaded up a car with the things she needed to take to college for her senior year and drove from Newnan to LaGrange.

When we got to the outskirts of LaGrange, I knew this was going to be the beginning of us being apart for a long time. I was very sad. I knew we were about to get to LaGrange College, and then events would happen automatically.

I said, "Julie, I don't want to wait a year to get married. I don't want to be apart from you for most of this year. I want us to get married right now."

I didn't know what she would say. I was sad and scared. I can't remember exactly what Julie said, but she must have seen how much I needed her. We turned the car around and drove back to Newnan.

As scared as I had been of her unpacking her stuff at LaGrange College, the minute she agreed with me and we headed back to Newnan, I was afraid of what her parents would say. I'm sure they wanted her to finish college. I was afraid they would be angry with me. I didn't know what I would do if they said she had to go back to college. I was really dreading going into her house and telling her parents.

However, they could not have been nicer. It was like they were expecting this to happen. Later I found out that they, themselves, had eloped when Julie's daddy was a student at Georgia Tech. His daddy had made him leave school and get a job. Maybe they remembered how they felt then. At any rate, they could not have been more calm or kind.

We all started trying to figure out how to make everything work. We decided that I would transfer from Washington and Lee to the University of Georgia in Athens. Fall classes there started the week of September 21. The best I can surmise is that this happened on August 16.

We decided the wedding would be on Saturday night, September 19, 1970, at the Central Baptist Church in Newnan. This meant there was no time to waste. In fact, there were less than five weeks before the wedding.

I remember that right after we told Julie's parents, Julie's momma set up a card table in their living room. All of us started planning everything and making lists of things to do and invitations to send out.

Julie's daddy asked Julie if she wanted to transfer from LaGrange College to Georgia and finish college there. However, Julie said she wanted to get a job to help us pay our bills.

I had to apply to the University of Georgia, Julie had to find a job in Athens, we had to find an apartment in Athens, the furniture we would use in our apartment had to be moved to Athens, and everything that went into preparing for a wedding had to be done in less than five weeks. Obviously, Julie and I could never have done all that on our own. The truth is that Julie, her momma, and her daddy did most of the work and deserve most of the credit for getting everything done.

The day after we decided to get married on September 19, I went back to work at the Jimmy Carter for Governor Headquarters in Atlanta. As often happens in political campaigns, the campaign was running low on money.

Hamilton Jordan, with whom I had roomed in both of Jimmy Carter's campaigns for governor in 1966 and that year and who was the campaign manager, called a meeting of the campaign staff. He said the campaign was short of money and asked us all to work without pay until the Democratic primary.

Everybody agreed to do this, except me. I said I had a clear understanding that I was to be paid a certain amount for my work on the campaign. I told them I was getting married in a few weeks and had to make some money in the meantime. I said I would have to leave the campaign and return to Fort Valley to work at the Blue Bird Bus Company until I got married, if Blue Bird would give me a job. That's what I did.

I have a letter I wrote to Julie from Fort Valley on Monday, August 24.

> Monday Night, Aug. 24, 1970
> Fort Valley, Ga.
>
> Dear Julie,
>
> I have just completed my first day here at Blue Bird and am typing this in Daddy's office while waiting for him to get ready to go home.
> Today was pretty good for a day at Blue Bird, and my job isn't as hard or as dull as I thought it might be. Anyway, I go through the whole day happy just because I keep thinking that in just four weeks we'll be married. I'm so excited and so happy about that!
> Last night it rained all the way from Newnan to Fort Valley. I drove carefully and slowly and every time I found myself going a few miles too fast, I could hear you telling me to slow down...

so I did. You are really making a better driver out of me.

I talked to the Carter people in Atlanta today. They were very nice to me, and I told them I was mad at the organization...but not mad at anybody. There are some nice folks who work there, and I want to keep them as our friends for years to come. Everybody I talked to at the headquarters said they had gotten their invitations to our wedding, and they all said they were coming. They also invited us to a Sunday meeting like the one we went to before this Sunday at 3:30. They wanted us both to come. I told them that we were on a tight schedule with me working 6 days a week here and with you working 7 days a week on the wedding, and that we probably wouldn't be able to attend the meeting. Still, if we're in Atlanta or don't have anything else to do, it's something to think about. Anyway, it was nice of them to invite us.

Momma and Sally went to Warner Robins this afternoon to buy Momma a dress for the wedding. Everybody's getting excited about it. (The wedding, not the dress.) They also said that when you go to clean up the apartment, they'd be glad to drive over and help if you want them to. Sally wanted to know what day you were coming this week and was disappointed when I told her that you probably wouldn't be able to come this week. They all enjoy seeing you so much and hope that you can come soon. If it is possible for you to come this week, please call and say so. We'd love to have you. If not this week, please come for a little visit in both of the next two weeks until I get through working here. I miss you a lot and would like nothing better than to see you right now.

As I said before, I was only hired here on a week-to-week basis. So I might not be here for the whole three weeks, but I probably will. Anyway, before we know it these four weeks will be over, and we'll be in Athens together forever. When I got home last night and walked in the door, I didn't feel like I was home at all. I know that now home for me is wherever we are together. I will not be home again until we move into our place in Athens, and I am surely looking forward to that blessed day!

I hope your parents are fine and that your mother is getting over her sickness. I know that cough is hard on her. Tell them hello for me. I think of them like my own parents.

Most of all, I hope you are feeling fine. Let me know if you're not. Call anytime to tell me anything, because whatever's on your mind is important to me.

I'm sorry this letter is so messy but I was never a good typist.

I love you and live for the day so near in the future when we will begin our life together in our own home. I think of you all the time and miss you and will see you soon. I have never been happier, and my happiness grows with every passing second which brings September 19 closer. Take care of yourself and God bless us always. I love you.

Love,
Steve

P.S.—
I love you so much!

To me, that letter seemed a lot less insecure than the ones I wrote Julie while she was on her trip. It sounds like I was no longer wondering if she was going to change her mind, at least not as much as I had earlier in our engagement.

That people had already received their invitations to our wedding meant that, somehow, in one week, the invitations had been printed, mailed out, and received by the people who had been invited. That is amazing to me.

I remember that we got so many nice wedding presents. Mr. and Mrs. Carter gave us a beautiful silver serving tray.

Julie's daddy was a well-respected man in Georgia. He was on the Board of Directors of Coca-Cola, the Atlanta and West Point Railroad, and some banks. He knew a lot of people. He called the president of the First National Bank of Athens and asked if he would consider giving Julie a job. Julie and her daddy went to Athens to meet him, and he gave Julie a job at the bank.

I especially remember the day we took a lot of things for our apartment from Newnan to Athens. That first year, we lived at the Oglethorpe Village Apartments. I can still see them. The building was two stories high with eight apartment units, and our little apartment was the third one from the left on the second floor.

As we moved everything in, we realized how symbolic it was when we set up Julie's bed, which she had slept in all her life. We knew it would be our bed soon. That told us that this apartment really was going to be our home. We still sleep in that same bed today.

Another great memory occurred on Saturday, September 12, 1970. That afternoon, we went to Atlanta to see my favorite team, the Georgia Tech Yellow Jackets, play a football game against the South Carolina Gamecocks. Tech came from behind to win in the fourth quarter. We sat in the North End Zone. Then, we had a special evening together.

Our engagement was brief, but it was wonderful and important. We grew much closer than we had been the night we were engaged. God used those special weeks to prepare us to be married.

Every day of the week of the wedding was special. I stayed at Julie's welcoming Aunt Annie's house, which was right between Julie's house and Matt Cole's house. The room I stayed in had a window looking out at the side of Julie's house. I remember looking through that window like it was yesterday.

I made up a game based on bowling using two dice that I played to help me go to sleep every night I slept there.

Oh, how I wanted that week to be over with so that Julie and I could move to Athens and start living in our apartment, away from all the relatives and the other people and events surrounding the wedding.

Somehow, everything we needed to accomplish was accomplished. Soon, it was the day for our wedding. What an amazing summer that had been. I am sure it was all because, for some reason I don't claim to fully understand, it was God's plan for Julie and me to get married.

> God is not a man, so He does not lie. He is not human, so He does not change His mind. Has He ever spoken and failed to act? Has He ever promised and not carried it through? (Numbers 23:19 NLT)

17 THE WEDDING

On Friday night, September 18, 1970, there was a rehearsal dinner at the Newnan Country Club. The main thing I remember from that event was that Momma and Daddy introduced me to the lady from the orphanage in South Carolina who had helped them when they adopted me twenty years before.

This will sound odd, but that surprised me. I always thought that I might have been Momma and Daddy's biological child, and they might have said I was adopted to keep from hurting my younger sister's feelings, since I knew she was adopted. That is insane, but for some reason, that's all I remember about that dinner. I guess it shows how sensitive I was about being adopted.

The next day, we had a lunch for everybody at the Newnan Country Club. Georgia Tech was hosting Florida State in a football game in Atlanta that afternoon. I asked some of my friends who were going to be in the wedding to pretend to kidnap me after this lunch.

My plan was that we could all go to the Tech game and get back in plenty of time for the wedding. Well, they kidnapped me, just like we planned, but they didn't take me to the football game. They took me out in the country and dumped me. I walked to a farmer's house. I knocked on his door and explained what had happened. He invited me in, and we watched Tech beat FSU on his TV.

After the game was over, I thanked the farmer and walked back to the road, where my friends had left me. About then, they came by, picked me up, and took me to the Holiday Inn just outside of Newnan, where our family was staying. I got dressed in my tuxedo. An old friend I hadn't seen in many years, Amy Flannigan, came by to say hello.

Then, Daddy and I drove to the Central Baptist Church. My daddy was my best man. On our drive to the church, Daddy started to explain to me what I should do on our wedding night. I told him I thought I had a general idea about what to do. I surely didn't want to talk about that. I was already nervous enough about the wedding.

Julie's brother, Ed Cole III, was an usher-groomsman, and so were two of my cousins, Lewis Henderson and Mike Moyer. The others were Matt Cole, Tom Cleveland, my best friend from Fort Valley, and Brad Sears, my best friend from Newnan.

Julie's best friend, Julie Power, was her maid of honor, and my sister, Sally, was one of Julie's bridesmaids. The other bridesmaids were Julie's close friends Lynda Osterman and Susan Neville. Another of Julie's best friends from LaGrange College, Angela Wise, kept the bride's book. It was a beautiful wedding.

Julie was, as the paper said, "given in marriage" by her father. Julie told me that, right before they walked down the aisle, her daddy asked her if she was sure this was what she wanted to do, and she told him she was.

Julie selected two songs that she wanted sung by a soloist at the wedding. They were "O Perfect Love" and "Walk Hand in Hand with Me."

Julie wrote our wedding vows herself, which are as follows.

> In linking my life with yours, I do not give up my
> cherished freedom, but rather I find freedom in
> you. To serve God as one with you, to follow you,
> to stand by you, and to love you is my supreme

purpose on this earth. With this ring I, Julie, wed thee, Steve.

In striving to build a home for you and in seeking God's will for our lives, I have found great purpose. To fulfill your needs, to care for you, and to love you is my supreme purpose on this earth. With this ring I, Steve, wed thee, Julie.

Julie also selected a scripture to be included.

And He answered and said unto them, "have ye not read, that He which made them at the beginning made them male and female, and said, for this cause shall a man leave father and mother, and shall cleave to his wife: and the twain shall be one flesh? Wherefore they are no more twain, but one flesh. What therefore God hath joined together, let not man put asunder." (Matthew 19:4–6)

After the preacher said I could kiss the bride, I gave Julie a hard and long kiss. I just wanted everybody to see how I felt about her.

As you can see from those vows and in that scripture, we were always conscious of the fact that God had done many miracles to bring us from that day in 1962, when I first saw Julie from the top of the steps of Newnan Junior High School and heard God speak the nine words about her to me, to the day we got married eight years later in 1970. God had fulfilled what He had told me in those nine words.

One of my favorite pictures is of us walking up the aisle to the door of the church after the wedding. Julie looked happy, and I looked determined to take her away with me as soon as I could.

After the wedding, there was a reception in the fellowship hall, complete with a giant wedding cake. Soon, we changed clothes and left for our thirty-six-hour honeymoon at the Holiday Inn at Callaway Gardens at Pine Mountain, Georgia.

When we left there that Monday morning, Julie wrote a postcard to her parents, which I have had framed, along with the newspaper's nice articles about our engagement announcement and our wedding. Julie's postcard read:

Monday

Dear Mother & Daddy,

We have really enjoyed our short rest here but are anxious to get home to Athens.

Hope you are getting your deserved rest too.

Much love,
Julie & Steve

But Ruth said, "Do not urge me to leave you or to return from following you. For where you go I will go, and where you lodge I will lodge. Your people shall be my people, and your God my God. Where you die, I will die, and there I will be buried. May the Lord do so to me and more also if anything but death parts me from you." (Ruth 1:16–17 ESV)

18 | NEWLYWEDS

As special as our wedding day, September 19, 1970, was, the following Monday, September 21, 1970, may have been even more special, at least to me. That was the day that we got past all the excitement and hectic preparation that led from that magic week in June, when we got engaged, to our wedding and our thirty-six-hour honeymoon.

Then, finally, we got to the thing I had been waiting for the entire time, to the "Promised Land" of beginning to live together in our own home.

When we got to Athens that Monday afternoon, the first thing we did was go to the grocery store near our apartment. I remember pushing the cart, while Julie selected the items she wanted to buy. I particularly remember that she bought a box of Noodles Almandine and Rice-A-Roni, known on TV ads back then as "the San Francisco Treat."

When we got married, I had no idea if Julie even knew how to cook at all, and it would not have mattered to me if she hadn't. It turned out that, from that first supper that Monday night, which was the first time I ever tasted her cooking, she was the greatest cook I ever knew.

I am not exaggerating one bit. My momma was a good cook, but Julie put Momma's cooking to shame. Here we are, over fifty-one years later, and she has still never cooked one meal that wasn't fabulous.

I've asked her how she learned to cook. She doesn't like questions like that. She says she just learned as she went. However, her cooking was too good from that first meal for me to be able to believe that.

Julie was always an excellent housekeeper. As a little girl, she had a little one-room house in her back yard that she cleaned every morning. She was so dedicated to doing this that her momma had to tell her not to use so many paper towels. Julie has always kept every place we lived as clean and nice as anyone could.

When you walked in the door of our apartment, you were

facing the table at which we ate, and our kitchen was behind that. To the right was the room I called our den, where we had our sitting chairs, sofa, and a black and white television.

Behind that was our bedroom and bathroom. It was wonderful. I would almost give my soul if God would let us go back to the day we moved into this wonderful little home and started our life together young, healthy, and happy.

Athens is a pretty town in a part of Georgia that has the four distinct seasons of the year. Every night after supper, we would go for a long walk, holding hands and talking and laughing the whole way.

I remember that every night on our walk we would pass by a retired couple in their yard, and an older lady in her yard. We spoke to these people every night and they were very kind to us.

It was cool in Athens after supper in the fall. I remember Julie wearing a gold or beige overcoat, a blouse, black pantyhose, and some bright yellow and red fall-colored checkered culottes.

When we got on the home stretch of the walk, I would say, "Let your nose lead the family." She would stick her nose out toward our apartment, and we would laugh our way home.

A funny thing she would say on these walks was, "What you got on…your mind?" When we got home, we would watch TV. Some of the shows I remember we watched that fall were

Marcus Welby, M.D., All in the Family, Hawaii Five-O, Ironside, The Carol Burnett Show, Mission: Impossible, and *The Mary Tyler Moore Show.*

The Mary Tyler Moore Show held a special place in our hearts, since its debut episode had been broadcast at the exact date and time we were married.

Julie's job at the First National Bank of Athens and my classes as a junior at the University of Georgia both started a few days after we moved into our apartment.

I can remember how Julie would spend several hours every night for what seemed like a long time writing thank you notes to all the people who had given us wedding presents while we watched TV.

Julie has always been a conscientious person. When there was a task that needed to be done, she did it. She did it quietly, caringly, and without wanting any credit for anything she did.

At the bank, Julie did a variety of jobs. Some days, she operated the telephone switchboard. Some days she would be checking the signatures on checks and filing them.

When I picked her up at the bank and we got home, she would be worn out, and her back would be very sore. I remember rubbing her shoulders, neck, and back to try to ease her pain.

We joined the First Baptist Church of Athens, which had

a preacher we really liked, Dr. Julian Cave. We would go to Sunday school and the eleven o'clock service, and then go back for the evening service.

We also liked going to the movies. In fact, when our first Christmas came along, we decided to stay in Athens, because Julie only had one day besides Christmas off from the bank. That Christmas day, we went to a nearly empty movie theatre and watched a triple feature of *Planet of the Apes* movies.

Every month, we went to Newnan to Julie's parents' house for one weekend and to Fort Valley to my parents' house for another weekend. That left us with only two or three weekends a month at home in Athens. Nevertheless, we had a great time.

Those were golden days. God had granted everything I asked Him for in that two-hour prayer back in 1962. He had to do a lot of miracles for me to get to marry Julie, but He did them. I am extremely happy and very thankful that He did.

Well, that's the story of *The Nine Words*. I believe that God told me to write it, and I wrote it the best I could. I guess if God wants to use it to help other people, He will have to do two more miracles. They would be getting it published and making it powerful to the people who read it. I don't know if He will. I just know that I wrote it as good as I could.

"Know therefore that the Lord your God is God; He is the faithful God, keeping his covenant of love to a thousand generations of those who love him and keep his commandments." (Deuteronomy 7:9 NIV)